The Book of Knowledge

A Journey Through Fascinating Facts, Strange Phenomena, and Odd Curiosities

By Gerald H. Rowden

Table of Contents

Dedication:..4
Chapter 1: Weird Science...4
Chapter 2: Peculiar History..7
Chapter 3: Fun with Food...11
Chapter 4: Uncommon Animals...14
Chapter 5: The Human Body: Stranger Than Fiction............18
Chapter 6: Mysteries of the Mind..22
Chapter 7: Geographic Oddities...26
Chapter 8: Laws That Make You Go "Huh?".........................30
Chapter 9: Inventions You Won't Believe Exist....................34
Chapter 9: Inventions You Won't Believe Exist....................35
Chapter 10: Language Wonders...38
Chapter 11: Strange Superstitions...42
Chapter 12: Eccentric Art and Literature...............................46
Chapter 13: Space Mysteries and Oddities............................51
Chapter 14: Unexplained Phenomena.....................................56
Chapter 15: Bizarre Sports and Games..................................61
Chapter 16: Human Curiosities..65
Conclusion: The Endless Curiosity of the World..................70

With a curious mind and a passion for learning, Gerald H. Rowden invites readers on a captivating journey into the realms of unusual knowledge. From rare phenomena and quirky inventions to historical oddities and unexplained mysteries, this book is a celebration of curiosity and the endless pursuit of understanding the world around us.

Dedication:

To all those who are endlessly curious, forever seeking the odd and unexplained wonders that make life so captivating.

Chapter 1: Weird Science

Bizarre Animal Behavior

- **Tardigrades** can survive extreme temperatures, radiation, and even the vacuum of space by entering a state called **cryptobiosis**.
- **Bowerbirds** build elaborate structures decorated with colorful objects to attract mates, arranging items by size and color.
- **Dolphins** have been observed using **pufferfish toxins** to induce a trance-like state, possibly getting themselves "high."
- **Opossums** play dead when threatened, even emitting a foul odor to convince predators they're already decaying.
- The **immortal jellyfish** can reverse its aging process and transform back into its juvenile form, effectively cheating death.

Weird Physics

- **Quantum entanglement**: Two particles can be instantly connected, regardless of distance, meaning an action on one affects the other even across vast distances.
- **Schrödinger's Cat**: In quantum mechanics, a cat in a box is both alive and dead until observed, highlighting the strange nature of quantum states.

- **Time dilation**: As you approach the speed of light, time slows down for you relative to someone standing still. Astronauts on the International Space Station age slightly slower than people on Earth.
- **Negative mass**: In theory, negative mass exists and would move in the opposite direction when pushed—a concept that still baffles scientists.
- **Spooky action at a distance**: Albert Einstein described quantum entanglement this way, struggling with the idea that particles could influence each other faster than the speed of light.

Curious Medical Trivia

- **Placebo effect**: In some cases, people improve after taking a fake treatment simply because they believe it's real.
- **Human teeth** are just as strong as shark teeth, despite their appearance and size differences.
- **Laughter** can increase blood flow by up to 20%, making it surprisingly good for your heart.
- **Synesthesia**: Some people can "hear" colors or "taste" sounds, as their senses are cross-wired in unusual ways.
- **Phantom limb syndrome**: After an amputation, some people still feel sensations, including pain, in the missing

Oddities in Biology

- **Axolotls** can regenerate entire limbs, including parts of their brain and heart, making them a unique subject of scientific study.
- **The wood frog** can survive being frozen solid during winter, stopping its heartbeat and all bodily functions until it thaws in the spring.

- **Hagfish** produce large amounts of slime as a defense mechanism, which can expand up to 10,000 times its original volume in water.
- **Octopuses** have three hearts and blue blood, due to a copper-based molecule (hemocyanin) used to transport oxygen.
- **The immortal jellyfish** (Turritopsis dohrnii) can revert back to its juvenile form after reaching adulthood, potentially living forever.

Strange Astronomical Phenomena

- **Diamond rain**: On planets like Neptune and Uranus, scientists believe that extreme pressure causes carbon to crystallize, creating literal diamond rain.
- **Rogue planets**: These are planets that don't orbit any star, drifting freely through space without a solar system to call home.
- **Pulsars**: These rapidly spinning neutron stars emit beams of radiation, and from Earth, they seem to "pulse" at regular intervals like cosmic lighthouses.
- **The Great Attractor**: A mysterious gravitational anomaly pulling entire galaxies, including our own, toward it at incomprehensible speeds, yet we can't see what it is.
- **Dark matter**: Though invisible and undetectable by current methods, dark matter makes up about 85% of the universe's mass and plays a key role in its structure.

Chapter 2: Peculiar History
Little-Known Historical Figures

- **Emperor Norton**: A self-proclaimed "Emperor of the United States" in the 19th century, Joshua Norton roamed the streets of San Francisco issuing decrees, which locals humorously followed.
- **Mary Anning**: A pioneering fossil hunter in the early 1800s, Anning discovered numerous important dinosaur fossils, though her contributions went largely unrecognized during her lifetime.
- **Simo Häyhä**: Known as the "White Death," this Finnish sniper holds the record for the most confirmed sniper kills (over 500) in history, during the Winter War between Finland and the Soviet Union.
- **Julie d'Aubigny**: A 17th-century French opera singer and swordswoman, she lived a life of duels, romance, and scandal, becoming a legend for her daring adventures.
- **Yasuke**: An African man who became a samurai in Japan in the late 1500s. Yasuke served under the famous warlord Oda Nobunaga, making him one of the few known non-Japanese samurai.

Odd Inventions and Their Creators

- **The Slinky**: Invented by accident in 1943 by **Richard James**, a naval engineer, when a spring fell off a shelf and "walked" across the floor, sparking the idea for this iconic toy.

- **The Baby Cage**: In the 1930s, **Emma Read** designed a cage that could be attached to apartment windows, allowing babies to get fresh air while suspended several stories high.
- **The Ice Cream Cone**: At the 1904 World's Fair, ice cream vendor **Ernest Hamwi** quickly rolled up a waffle when another vendor ran out of dishes, creating the first ice cream cone.
- **The Pet Rock**: In 1975, **Gary Dahl** sold smooth rocks in a box as pets, complete with an instruction manual. This simple joke became a massive fad, making him a millionaire.
- **The Great Stink Solution**: In 1858, engineer **Joseph Bazalgette** designed London's underground sewer system in response to the "Great Stink," a summer when the Thames became so polluted it forced Parliament to act.

Strange Historical Coincidences

- **Lincoln and Kennedy**: Both U.S. Presidents were shot on a Friday, seated next to their wives. Lincoln's secretary was named Kennedy, and Kennedy's secretary was named Lincoln. Both assassins were known by their full names and were killed before trial.
- **Edgar Allan Poe's "The Narrative of Arthur Gordon Pym"**: Poe's 1838 novel describes shipwreck survivors who resort to cannibalism. In 1884, a real shipwreck occurred, and the survivors, who cannibalized a cabin boy, eerily shared the same name as Poe's fictional victim: Richard Parker.
- **The Battle of Waterloo and a volcanic eruption**: The massive eruption of Mount Tambora in 1815 caused climate abnormalities, which led to wet and muddy conditions at

the Battle of Waterloo in 1815. Some historians speculate that the weather impacted Napoleon's defeat.
- **The Hoover Dam tragedy**: The first and last workers to die during the construction of the Hoover Dam were father and son: **J.G. Tierney** and **Patrick Tierney**. Both died exactly 13 years apart on December 20.
- **Titanic and the novel "Futility"**: In 1898, 14 years before the Titanic sank, author **Morgan Robertson** wrote "Futility," a novel about a ship named Titan that hits an iceberg and sinks. Both ships were described as "unsinkable."

Bizarre Battles and Wars
- **The War of the Stray Dog (1925)**: This conflict between Greece and Bulgaria started when a Greek soldier chased his dog across the border, leading to gunfire. The brief war ended with Greece paying reparations.
- **The Pig War (1859)**: A conflict between the U.S. and Britain started when an American farmer shot a British-owned pig that wandered into his garden on San Juan Island. The two nations almost went to war, but no human casualties occurred.
- **The Emu War (1932)**: In Australia, military soldiers were sent to control an emu population wreaking havoc on crops. The emus proved too fast and agile, leading to a humiliating military withdrawal, with the emus "winning" the war.
- **The Football War (1969)**: A brief war between El Salvador and Honduras broke out after tensions from a football match during the World Cup qualifiers. The match itself

didn't cause the war but heightened already existing tensions.
- **The Battle of the Golden Stool (1900)**: The British Empire clashed with the Ashanti Empire in Ghana over a sacred stool that symbolized the Ashanti's soul. Despite the British winning, they never captured the stool, which remains an important symbol to the Ashanti people today.

Quirky Moments from Ancient Civilizations

- **The Roman vomitorium myth**: Contrary to popular belief, vomitoria were not rooms where Romans went to vomit between feasts. They were actually passageways in amphitheaters for quick exits.
- **The Egyptian love of cats**: Ancient Egyptians revered cats so highly that killing one, even accidentally, could be punishable by death. They believed cats were sacred and embodied the goddess Bastet.
- **King Tut's dagger**: A dagger found in the tomb of King Tutankhamun was made from meteorite iron, showing that ancient Egyptians valued celestial objects in their craftsmanship.
- **Greek "ostracism" punishment**: In ancient Athens, citizens could vote to exile someone for 10 years. They wrote the person's name on a piece of pottery (ostrakon). It was an early form of democratic punishment.
- **Aztec sacrifices**: The Aztecs believed their gods needed nourishment from human blood, so they performed regular sacrifices. However, some evidence suggests the practice may not have been as common as earlier believed.

Chapter 3: Fun with Food

Strange Delicacies from Around the World

- **Casu marzu (Italy)**: This Sardinian cheese is notorious for being filled with live maggots. The larvae help ferment the cheese, which is eaten while the maggots are still wriggling inside.
- **Balut (Philippines)**: A fertilized duck egg with a partially developed embryo inside, balut is boiled and eaten directly from the shell. It's considered a delicacy and a common street food.
- **Hákarl (Iceland)**: This Icelandic dish is made from fermented shark meat, which is buried and left to ferment for several months. The meat has a strong ammonia smell and is often described as an acquired taste.
- **Fugu (Japan)**: This potentially deadly delicacy is made from pufferfish, which contains lethal toxins. Only specially trained and licensed chefs are allowed to prepare it, as one wrong cut could be fatal.
- **Escamoles (Mexico)**: Known as "insect caviar," escamoles are the larvae of ants harvested from the roots of agave plants. They are often served in tacos or with guacamole and have a nutty, buttery flavor.

Surprising Food Origins

- **Ketchup**: Originally, ketchup was made from fermented fish brine in China. It wasn't until the 1800s that tomatoes became the main ingredient, creating the ketchup we know today.
- **Chocolate**: The ancient Mayans and Aztecs believed chocolate was a gift from the gods. However, their version

of chocolate was bitter and consumed as a spiced drink, not the sweet treat we enjoy today.
- **Potatoes**: Native to the Andes Mountains in South America, potatoes were once believed to be poisonous in Europe because they are part of the deadly nightshade family. It took centuries for them to be accepted as a staple food.
- **Pineapples**: Pineapples were once so rare and expensive in Europe that they were rented out for parties and used as status symbols rather than eaten.
- **Caesar Salad**: Despite its Italian-sounding name, Caesar salad was invented by Italian-American chef **Caesar Cardini** in Mexico during the 1920s when he ran out of ingredients and threw together what he had on hand.

Weird Food Laws

- **No margarine in Wisconsin (USA)**: Until recently, it was illegal to serve margarine in Wisconsin restaurants unless the customer specifically asked for it, a law designed to protect the state's dairy industry.
- **No fish on Sundays in Ohio (USA)**: It's illegal to get a fish drunk in Ohio, an odd law that dates back to the 1800s, though how one would get a fish intoxicated remains a mystery.
- **France's bread laws**: In France, a law passed in 1993 regulates that traditional baguettes must only contain four ingredients: flour, water, yeast, and salt. Anything else, and it's not a true baguette.

- **No watermelon in public**: In one Australian town, eating watermelon in public is forbidden to prevent littering from the discarded rinds.
- **No garlic after 6 p.m. in Italy**: In some parts of Italy, it was once illegal to eat garlic after 6 p.m. because it was believed the smell lingered too strongly for evening social events.

Bizarre Eating Competitions

- **Nathan's Hot Dog Eating Contest (USA)**: Every 4th of July, competitive eaters gather at Coney Island to see who can eat the most hot dogs in 10 minutes. The current record is 76 hot dogs, held by **Joey Chestnut**.
- **The World Pie Eating Championship (UK)**: Held in Wigan, England, this competition challenges participants to eat a meat and potato pie as fast as possible. Speed is prioritized over quantity, with a focus on quick bites.
- **The Stinging Nettle Eating Championship (UK)**: Contestants chew through as many feet of stinging nettles as they can in one hour. They're judged on how much leaf they consume while enduring the painful stings.
- **Krystal Burger Eating Contest (USA)**: Competitors race to consume as many small Krystal burgers as they can. In 2019, **Carmen Cincotti** set a record by eating 103 burgers in 8 minutes.
- **The World Oyster Eating Championship (Ireland)**: In this challenge, contestants see who can swallow the most oysters in just three minutes. Some competitors consume hundreds of oysters in that short period.

Unusual Food Inventions

- **Square Watermelons (Japan)**: These specially grown watermelons are cultivated inside square boxes, allowing them to grow into a cube shape. Originally designed to fit neatly in refrigerators, they are now sold as luxury items.
- **Glow-in-the-dark ice cream**: Created using jellyfish proteins, this unusual dessert glows as you lick it. It's an innovative (and expensive) treat from British inventor **Charlie Francis**.
- **Instant noodles**: Invented by **Momofuku Ando** in 1958, instant noodles became a worldwide sensation. Ando created them during food shortages in Japan to offer a quick and affordable meal option.
- **The Ramen Burger**: In 2013, chef **Keizo Shimamoto** replaced burger buns with crispy ramen noodles, creating a fusion food that became an instant hit at food festivals.
- **Kopi Luwak (Indonesia)**: Known as "civet coffee," this rare drink is made from coffee beans that have been eaten and passed by civet cats. The beans undergo fermentation in the animal's digestive system, resulting in a unique flavor.

Chapter 4: Uncommon Animals

Rare and Endangered Species

- **Vaquita (Mexico)**: This small porpoise is critically endangered, with fewer than 10 individuals left in the wild. Found only in the northern part of the Gulf of California, vaquitas are threatened by illegal fishing nets.

- **Amur Leopard (Russia and China)**: With fewer than 100 left in the wild, the Amur leopard is one of the rarest big cats. These leopards live in the forests of the Russian Far East and are known for their incredible speed and agility.
- **Axolotl (Mexico)**: This "walking fish" is not a fish at all but a type of salamander. It is endangered due to habitat loss, pollution, and invasive species in the waterways of Mexico City.
- **Saola (Vietnam and Laos)**: Often called the "Asian unicorn" due to its elusiveness, the saola is one of the rarest animals in the world, discovered only in 1992. It lives in the forests along the Laos-Vietnam border.
- **Northern White Rhino (Africa)**: Only two northern white rhinos remain, both of them female. Conservationists are working on advanced reproductive technologies to try and save the species from extinction.

Animals with Superpowers

- **The Tardigrade**: Known as the "water bear," tardigrades can survive extreme conditions, including temperatures close to absolute zero, intense radiation, and even the vacuum of space by entering a state called cryptobiosis.
- **Mantis Shrimp**: With one of the fastest punches in the animal kingdom, mantis shrimp can strike with the force of a bullet, capable of cracking shells and even aquarium glass.
- **The Immortal Jellyfish (Turritopsis dohrnii)**: This jellyfish can revert back to its juvenile state after reaching adulthood, essentially resetting its life cycle and potentially living forever.

- **Pistol Shrimp**: This small shrimp snaps its claw so quickly that it creates a bubble capable of stunning prey and producing temperatures nearly as hot as the surface of the sun.
- **The Bombardier Beetle**: When threatened, the bombardier beetle ejects a boiling hot chemical spray from its abdomen, making it one of the most effective defense mechanisms in the insect world.

Unusual Animal Partnerships

- **The Oxpecker and Large Mammals**: Oxpeckers are small birds that ride on the backs of animals like rhinos, giraffes, and buffalo. They eat parasites and dead skin from their hosts, while getting a free meal and protection from predators.
- **The Clownfish and Sea Anemone**: Clownfish are immune to the stings of sea anemones, which protect them from predators. In return, clownfish help keep the anemone clean and lure food into its tentacles.
- **Cleaner Fish and Sharks**: Cleaner fish, like the cleaner wrasse, pick parasites and dead tissue from sharks' skin and gills. The sharks benefit from the cleaning, while the fish get a steady food source without being eaten.
- **Ants and Aphids**: Some species of ants "farm" aphids, protecting them from predators in exchange for a sugary substance called honeydew that the aphids secrete.
- **Crocodiles and Egyptian Plover Birds**: Although rare, some stories tell of the plover bird entering the open mouths of crocodiles to clean their teeth. The bird gets a meal, and the crocodile receives dental hygiene.

Animal Record Holders

- **Fastest Animal**: The **peregrine falcon** holds the record for the fastest animal, diving at speeds of over 240 mph (386 km/h) when hunting prey.
- **Largest Animal**: The **blue whale** is the largest animal to have ever existed, reaching lengths of up to 100 feet (30 meters) and weighing as much as 200 tons.
- **Smallest Mammal**: The **bumblebee bat** is the smallest mammal, weighing only about 2 grams (less than a penny) and measuring just over an inch long.
- **Oldest Living Creature**: The **quahog clam**, named Ming, was estimated to be 507 years old when it was discovered, making it the longest-lived animal known to science.
- **Loudest Animal**: The **sperm whale** produces clicks that can reach 230 decibels, making it the loudest sound of any animal on Earth—louder than a jet engine.

Strange Animal Behaviors

- **Dancing Spiders**: Male **peacock spiders** perform elaborate, colorful dances to attract females, waving their legs and bodies in intricate patterns.
- **Self-Decorating Crabs**: **Decorator crabs** cover their shells with algae, sponges, and other debris to blend into their surroundings and avoid predators.
- **Tool-Using Crows**: **New Caledonian crows** are known for using sticks and leaves as tools to extract insects from hard-to-reach places, showcasing their remarkable intelligence.
- **Puffin Beak Rubbing**: Puffins engage in a behavior called "billing," where they rub their colorful beaks together as part of courtship displays and bonding rituals.

- **Kleptoparasitic Seagulls**: Some **seagulls** specialize in stealing food from other birds, known as kleptoparasitism. They harass other birds until they drop their catch, then swoop in to steal it.

Chapter 5: The Human Body: Stranger Than Fiction
Rare Medical Conditions

- **Progeria**: A rare genetic disorder that causes children to age rapidly. Most people with progeria live only into their teens or early twenties, though their mental development remains unaffected.
- **Hyperthymesia**: People with this condition have an extraordinary ability to recall every detail of their lives. They can remember specific dates, conversations, and events from years ago, sometimes to the exact second.
- **Congenital Insensitivity to Pain**: People with this disorder can't feel physical pain, which might sound like a superpower, but it's dangerous. They can be unaware of injuries or infections, leading to severe complications.
- **Alien Hand Syndrome**: A condition where one hand seems to have a mind of its own, moving involuntarily and sometimes performing actions the person doesn't intend, such as grabbing objects or even attempting self-harm.
- **Foreign Accent Syndrome**: After a brain injury or stroke, some people suddenly start speaking with a different accent, even though they have never been to the region where the accent originates.

Unexplained Body Phenomena

- **Déjà vu**: The strange sensation that you've experienced something before, even though you know it's happening for the first time. The exact cause of déjà vu is still a mystery, though some researchers believe it's related to memory processing in the brain.
- **Goosebumps**: A reflex inherited from our ancestors, goosebumps occur when tiny muscles at the base of hair follicles contract, making the hairs stand up. In animals, this makes them appear larger when threatened; in humans, it's mostly useless.
- **Hiccups**: Caused by sudden contractions of the diaphragm, hiccups are a persistent and often inexplicable reflex. Despite being common, no definitive cure exists, and they can sometimes last for days or even years.
- **Sleep Paralysis**: A terrifying condition where people wake up but can't move or speak. This occurs when the body is still in the REM stage of sleep, leaving the person aware but paralyzed. Many also experience hallucinations during sleep paralysis.
- **Photic Sneeze Reflex**: About 18-35% of the population sneezes when suddenly exposed to bright light, such as walking outside on a sunny day. This reaction, known as the photic sneeze reflex, is still not fully understood by scientists.

Strange Records Set by Humans

- **Longest Fingernails**: **Lee Redmond** holds the record for the longest fingernails ever grown, with a combined length of 28 feet (8.65 meters) before she cut them in 2009.
- **Most Tattoos**: **Lucky Diamond Rich** has tattooed 100% of his body, including his eyelids, the insides of his mouth, and even his gums, making him the most tattooed person in the world.
- **Stretchiest Skin**: **Garry Turner**, who has a rare condition called Ehlers-Danlos syndrome, can stretch the skin of his stomach to over 6 inches (15 cm) due to his highly elastic skin.
- **Most Body Modifications**: **Rolf Buchholz** holds the record for the most body modifications, with over 516 alterations, including tattoos, piercings, implants, and scarification.
- **Longest Hair**: **Xie Qiuping** from China holds the record for the longest hair, which measures over 18 feet (5.6 meters). She has been growing her hair since 1973.

Unusual Facts About How We Perceive the World

- **The Nose Can Detect Trillions of Scents**: While people often say humans have a poor sense of smell compared to animals, recent studies suggest we can distinguish between over a trillion different odors.
- **Blind Spot in Vision**: Every human eye has a blind spot where the optic nerve passes through the retina. Your brain fills in the missing information, so you don't notice it in daily life.
- **Synesthesia**: Some people experience **synesthesia**, where their senses overlap. For example, they might "see" music as colors or "taste" certain words.

- **The McGurk Effect**: This phenomenon occurs when what you see affects what you hear. If you watch someone saying "ba" but the video shows "ga," your brain might hear "da" instead—proving how intertwined our senses are.
- **Color Doesn't Exist in the Dark**: When there's no light, your brain cannot perceive color. What we interpret as "black" in darkness is simply the absence of light.

Bizarre Bodily Functions

- **Sneezing While Sleeping**: It's impossible to sneeze while you're asleep because your body's reflexes are shut down during REM sleep, the stage where dreaming occurs.
- **Ears Never Stop Growing**: While bones stop growing after puberty, the soft cartilage in your ears (and nose) continues to grow throughout your life, making them larger as you age.
- **Fingernails Grow Faster on the Dominant Hand**: The nails on your dominant hand grow slightly faster than those on your non-dominant hand, likely because of increased blood flow and usage.
- **Stomach Growls**: The sound of your stomach growling, known as **borborygmi**, is caused by air and fluid moving through the intestines as they contract during digestion or when empty.
- **Yawning Is Contagious**: Seeing or even thinking about yawning can make you yawn. Scientists aren't entirely sure why, but it's believed to be linked to social bonding and empathy.

Chapter 6: Mysteries of the Mind

Optical Illusions and How They Trick Us

- **The Müller-Lyer Illusion**: In this illusion, two lines of equal length appear to be different lengths because of the arrows at their ends. The brain interprets the lines based on contextual clues, tricking you into seeing one as longer.
- **The Ames Room**: A distorted room designed to make objects or people appear to grow or shrink as they move around. This happens because the room's shape fools the brain into thinking everything is normal, even though the floor and walls are uneven.
- **The Checker Shadow Illusion**: In this optical illusion, a checkered board is placed in shadow, and two squares that appear to be different shades are actually the same color. The brain is tricked by the shadow and the context of the board's pattern.
- **The Kanizsa Triangle**: In this illusion, a triangle appears to exist in the center of three circles and three V shapes, even though no triangle is drawn. The brain fills in the gaps, perceiving a shape where there is none.
- **Motion Aftereffect**: After staring at a moving object for a while (like a waterfall), when you look away, stationary objects appear to move in the opposite direction. This happens because neurons that detect motion become fatigued and send reversed signals.

Weird Psychological Experiments

- **The Stanford Prison Experiment (1971)**: Psychologist **Philip Zimbardo** simulated a prison environment with volunteers as guards and prisoners. The "guards" quickly became abusive, demonstrating how easily people conform to roles of authority, leading to the experiment's early termination after just six days.
- **Little Albert Experiment (1920)**: Conducted by **John B. Watson**, this experiment conditioned a baby named Albert to fear fluffy objects by pairing them with loud, scary noises. It was an early demonstration of classical conditioning, though considered unethical today.
- **The Milgram Experiment (1961)**: **Stanley Milgram** studied obedience to authority by having participants administer what they believed were painful electric shocks to others. Many participants followed orders to the point of delivering potentially fatal shocks, revealing people's willingness to obey authority.
- **The Monster Study (1939)**: Researchers tested the effects of positive and negative reinforcement on stuttering in children. They gave some children praise for their speech, while others were criticized. The study, considered unethical, led to lasting emotional trauma for some participants.
- **The Bobo Doll Experiment (1961)**: **Albert Bandura** demonstrated that children imitate aggressive behavior by showing them adults attacking an inflatable doll. The children who observed the violence were more likely to exhibit aggressive actions toward the doll themselves.

Strange Mental Disorders

- **Cotard's Delusion**: A rare disorder where the person believes they are dead, missing parts of their body, or don't exist. Sufferers often experience extreme depression and may refuse to eat or care for themselves, believing it's unnecessary for a "dead" person.
- **Capgras Syndrome**: People with Capgras syndrome believe that someone close to them, often a family member or friend, has been replaced by an identical imposter. This delusion can create immense distrust and confusion in personal relationships.
- **Fregoli Delusion**: A condition where the affected person believes different people are actually the same individual in disguise. It's often associated with paranoid schizophrenia and can lead to severe anxiety.
- **Alice in Wonderland Syndrome**: Named after Lewis Carroll's book, this syndrome distorts a person's perception of size and distance. Objects or people may appear smaller or larger than they are, creating a disorienting experience.
- **Exploding Head Syndrome**: Despite its alarming name, this disorder causes people to hear a sudden, loud noise (like an explosion or gunshot) as they fall asleep or wake up. The sound is entirely imagined and isn't harmful, though it can be frightening.

Unusual Habits and Rituals from History

- **Mummifying Dead Royals in Honey (Ancient Egypt)**: In ancient Egypt, honey was used to mummify royalty and preserve their bodies. Honey's natural antibacterial properties helped prevent decay.
- **Napoleon's Strange Sleeping Schedule**: Napoleon Bonaparte reportedly slept in very short bursts, napping

throughout the day and night rather than sleeping in one long stretch. He believed this increased his productivity.
- **Victorian Mourning Rituals**: During the Victorian era, mourning the dead became an elaborate process. Women were expected to wear black for up to two years, and many families took post-mortem photographs of deceased relatives as keepsakes.
- **Roman Vomitoriums (Roman Empire)**: Contrary to popular belief, vomitoriums weren't rooms where Romans went to purge during feasts. They were large passageways designed to allow crowds to exit amphitheaters quickly after events.
- **The Habit of Eating Dirt (Geophagy)**: In various cultures throughout history, people practiced **geophagy**, the eating of dirt or clay. This ritual was believed to have medicinal or spiritual benefits, though it still occurs in some regions today for different reasons.

Quirky Brain Facts

- **The Brain Has No Pain Receptors**: While your brain processes pain, it doesn't feel pain itself. This is why brain surgery can be performed while a patient is awake, without the brain feeling any discomfort.
- **You Forget 90% of Your Dreams**: Within five minutes of waking up, most people forget a majority of their dreams. It's believed this happens because the brain is focused on transitioning to wakefulness and storing important memories.
- **Your Brain Runs on Electricity**: The brain generates enough electrical power to light a small LED bulb. Neurons

communicate using electrical impulses, making your brain a complex electrical system.
- **The Brain Shrinks Over Time**: As you age, your brain slowly shrinks, losing about 5-10% of its weight between the ages of 20 and 90. This shrinking is normal but can affect memory and cognitive function.
- **Your Brain Uses 20% of Your Body's Energy**: Despite making up only about 2% of your body weight, your brain consumes roughly 20% of your body's energy to fuel its constant activity.

Chapter 7: Geographic Oddities

Oddly-Shaped Countries and Islands

- **The Gambia**: Shaped like a thin strip of land, The Gambia follows the Gambia River for 295 miles. It's only about 30 miles wide, making it one of the narrowest countries in the world.
- **Cyprus**: Cyprus resembles a deformed teardrop with a long, jagged peninsula that extends from its northeast coast. The island's shape is unique among Mediterranean nations.
- **Svalbard (Norway)**: This remote archipelago in the Arctic is composed of oddly shaped islands with rugged, angular coastlines. Svalbard's largest island, Spitsbergen, looks like a spider with multiple "legs."
- **Lesotho**: Lesotho is an unusual country because it's completely landlocked and entirely surrounded by South Africa, making it one of the few countries in the world that's an enclave within another nation.

- **Kiribati**: Made up of 33 atolls spread across the Pacific Ocean, Kiribati's land area is dwarfed by the massive size of its ocean territory, giving it a sprawling and disjointed shape.

Bizarre Natural Formations

- **The Eye of the Sahara (Mauritania)**: Also known as the **Richat Structure**, this massive circular formation looks like a giant eye in the desert. Its concentric rings are about 25 miles in diameter and are visible from space.
- **The Wave (USA)**: Located in Arizona, The Wave is a swirling sandstone formation that looks like a painted ocean wave frozen in time. Its unique, undulating patterns are the result of millions of years of erosion.
- **Giant's Causeway (Northern Ireland)**: This striking formation consists of about 40,000 interlocking basalt columns, many of which are hexagonal. The result of an ancient volcanic eruption, it resembles a massive stone pathway.
- **Pamukkale (Turkey)**: Pamukkale, meaning "cotton castle" in Turkish, is famous for its white terraces formed by mineral-rich hot springs. The cascading pools of blue water make it look like a snowy landscape, even in the heat of summer.
- **Salar de Uyuni (Bolivia)**: The world's largest salt flat, Salar de Uyuni, is so vast and flat that during the rainy season, it reflects the sky like a perfect mirror, creating a surreal, otherworldly scene.

Rare Climates and Ecosystems

- **The Danakil Depression (Ethiopia)**: One of the hottest and most inhospitable places on Earth, this desert has temperatures reaching up to 125°F (52°C). It's dotted with boiling springs and acidic pools, creating a surreal, alien landscape.
- **The Atacama Desert (Chile)**: Known as the driest non-polar desert in the world, some parts of the Atacama haven't seen rainfall in hundreds of years. Despite the harsh environment, rare "flowering deserts" occur after rare rains, covering the area in blooms.
- **The Sundarbans (India and Bangladesh)**: The largest mangrove forest in the world, the Sundarbans is home to a unique ecosystem that includes salt-tolerant trees and a population of endangered Bengal tigers that swim between islands.
- **Socotra Island (Yemen)**: Isolated from the mainland for millions of years, Socotra has one of the most unique ecosystems on Earth. Over a third of its plant species, including the iconic dragon's blood tree, are found nowhere else in the world.
- **Oymyakon (Russia)**: Known as the coldest inhabited place on Earth, temperatures in Oymyakon can plummet to -88°F (-67°C). Despite this, people live here year-round, adapting to the brutal climate with special techniques for survival.

Strange Cities and Towns with Unusual Histories

- **Kolmanskop (Namibia)**: Once a bustling diamond mining town, Kolmanskop is now a ghost town, slowly being

swallowed by the desert. The empty houses, filled with drifting sand, create an eerie, abandoned landscape.
- **Coober Pedy (Australia)**: Known as the "underground town," Coober Pedy is famous for its opal mining. Due to the extreme heat, many residents live in homes dug into the ground to stay cool.
- **Miyake-jima (Japan)**: Located on an active volcano, residents of this island are required to carry gas masks at all times due to the constant risk of poisonous gas emissions. Despite the danger, people continue to live there.
- **Pripyat (Ukraine)**: Abandoned after the Chernobyl disaster in 1986, Pripyat remains frozen in time. The city, once home to 50,000 people, is now a haunting snapshot of life before the nuclear accident.
- **Hallstatt (Austria)**: A picturesque village known for its beauty, Hallstatt's replica was controversially built in China. The original town's history dates back to prehistoric times, and it has a long tradition of salt mining.

Curious Facts About the Earth's Extreme Locations

- **Mount Everest (Nepal/Tibet)**: The tallest mountain on Earth, Everest's summit stands at 29,032 feet (8,849 meters) above sea level. However, because of Earth's equatorial bulge, Mount Chimborazo in Ecuador is technically the farthest point from the Earth's center.
- **The Dead Sea (Jordan/Israel)**: The lowest point on Earth's surface, the Dead Sea sits 1,410 feet (430 meters) below sea level. It's also one of the saltiest bodies of water in the world, making it nearly impossible for life to thrive in it.

- **The Mariana Trench (Pacific Ocean)**: The deepest point in the Earth's oceans, the Mariana Trench reaches a depth of about 36,070 feet (10,994 meters). The pressure at this depth is more than 1,000 times atmospheric pressure at sea level.
- **Antarctica**: Not only is Antarctica the coldest place on Earth, but it also holds the record for the lowest temperature ever recorded: -128.6°F (-89.2°C) at the Vostok Station in 1983. The continent also contains 90% of the world's fresh water, locked in its ice sheets.
- **Salar de Uyuni (Bolivia)**: The world's largest salt flat, covering over 4,000 square miles (10,000 square kilometers), is so flat that NASA uses it to calibrate satellites. During the rainy season, it becomes the world's largest mirror.

Chapter 8: Laws That Make You Go "Huh?"
Weird Laws Around the World

- **No Chewing Gum in Singapore**: Since 1992, Singapore has banned the sale and import of chewing gum to keep the streets clean. Exceptions are made for medicinal gum, but strict fines are imposed for improper disposal.
- **No High Heels in Greece's Ancient Sites**: In Greece, wearing high heels at historical sites, such as the Acropolis, is prohibited. The law was introduced to protect the ancient stone structures from damage caused by sharp heels.
- **No Public Swearing in Australia**: In parts of Australia, swearing in public is illegal and can lead to hefty fines. Queensland and Victoria have especially strict rules, with potential fines of over $100.

- **You Must Smile in Milan (Italy)**: Milan has a law requiring people to smile at all times in public, except during funerals or hospital visits. This bizarre rule is rarely enforced but remains on the books.
- **No Feeding Pigeons in Venice (Italy)**: Venice has banned feeding pigeons in St. Mark's Square to reduce the damage the birds cause to historic buildings. Violators can face fines of up to €700.

Bizarre U.S. State Laws

- **Alabama**: It is illegal to wear a fake mustache that causes laughter in church. This quirky law aims to prevent disruptions during religious services.
- **Arizona**: You may not allow your donkey to sleep in a bathtub. This strange law was passed after a local flood caused a donkey sleeping in a tub to float away, requiring an expensive rescue operation.
- **Georgia**: It's illegal to eat fried chicken with a fork in Gainesville, Georgia. The law was originally intended as a humorous publicity stunt to promote the city as the "Poultry Capital of the World."
- **Nebraska**: In Lehigh, it is illegal to sell donut holes. The origin of this peculiar law is unclear, but it remains on the books, even though it's not enforced.
- **New York**: In New York City, it's illegal to wear slippers after 10 p.m. The reasoning behind this law is to prevent noise disturbances caused by people walking around late at night in loud or squeaky slippers.

Historical Laws and Punishments That Seem Absurd Today

- **Trial by Ordeal (Medieval Europe)**: In this judicial practice, the accused underwent painful or dangerous tests, such as holding hot iron or being submerged in water. If they survived or weren't injured, they were deemed innocent by divine intervention.
- **The Scold's Bridle (16th Century England)**: Women accused of gossiping or being "nagging wives" could be punished with a metal bridle that covered the head and inserted a spiked bit into the mouth to prevent talking.
- **Foot Binding (Ancient China)**: While not a law, foot binding was a cultural practice that forced women to have their feet tightly bound from a young age to achieve the "lotus foot" shape. The painful practice was outlawed in the early 20th century.
- **The Ducking Stool (Colonial America and Europe)**: Used to punish women accused of being witches or scolds, they were strapped to a chair and dunked into a body of water repeatedly as punishment or humiliation.
- **Sumptuary Laws (Renaissance Europe)**: These laws regulated what people could wear based on their social class. For example, commoners were forbidden from wearing purple, which was reserved for royalty and the nobility.

Unintended Consequences of Strange Laws

- **Prohibition (USA, 1920-1933)**: The 18th Amendment banned the sale and consumption of alcohol, but instead of eliminating drinking, it gave rise to bootlegging,

speakeasies, and organized crime. Figures like Al Capone flourished, and the law ultimately led to its repeal in 1933.
- **The Window Tax (England, 1696)**: A property tax based on the number of windows in a house led many people to brick up their windows to avoid paying. The law was eventually repealed in 1851, but many older buildings still have bricked-up windows today.
- **The Hat Tax (England, 1784-1811)**: A tax on hats resulted in people avoiding the tax by making headwear that couldn't legally be classified as hats. It also contributed to the rise of counterfeit tax stamps.
- **The Dog Muzzle Law (Switzerland, 1904)**: This law required all dogs to be muzzled in public to prevent rabies. However, it led to the unintended consequence of more stray dogs being abandoned by their owners to avoid the hassle.
- **The Chicken Ordinance (Brainerd, Minnesota, USA)**: A law meant to limit noise from chickens by mandating they be kept indoors after dark had the opposite effect—people brought more chickens indoors, creating more noise complaints from neighbors.

Curious Legal Loopholes

- **The Vatican and the Pirate Radio Station**: In the 1960s, Vatican City exploited an international loophole to run Radio Vaticana, broadcasting outside the control of Italian airwaves. Its powerful transmissions interfered with other frequencies, causing international disputes.
- **Beer Was Not Alcohol (Iceland, 1915-1989)**: During Iceland's alcohol ban, beer was classified separately and

wasn't included in the prohibition until the government realized the loophole. The ban on beer persisted until 1989.
- **Duty-Free Shopping (International Airports)**: Due to their unique location in international zones, duty-free shops in airports are not subject to local taxes. This legal loophole allows travelers to purchase items at lower prices without paying duties.
- **Prostitution in Nevada**: Prostitution is illegal in most U.S. states, but a legal loophole in Nevada permits it in rural counties with populations under 700,000. Brothels operate legally in these areas, despite state and federal bans elsewhere.
- **The Principality of Sealand**: A man named Paddy Roy Bates claimed an abandoned military platform off the coast of England in the 1960s, declaring it the independent Principality of Sealand. Despite multiple attempts to shut it down, Sealand exists in a legal gray area as a "micronation."

Chapter 9: Inventions You Won't Believe Exist
Absurd Patents from History

- **The Cat Mew Machine (1963)**: Patented in Japan, this device was designed to scare away mice by mimicking the sound of a cat's meow. It emitted periodic "mews" to keep pests at bay, though it never became widely popular.
- **The Anti-Eating Mask (1982)**: This invention was meant to help people lose weight by covering their mouth with a mask that only allowed liquids to pass through. It was patented in the U.S. but was never adopted as a weight-loss solution.

- **The Dog Umbrella (2005)**: Designed for dogs who dislike the rain, this umbrella attaches to the dog's leash, keeping them dry during walks. While it may seem practical, it never became a widespread product.
- **The Bird Diaper (1999)**: Created for pet owners who want to avoid bird droppings around the house, this diaper for birds caught waste in a small pouch. Despite its quirky idea, it failed to catch on in the pet market.
- **The Baby Cage (1922)**: This patent proposed a wire cage that could be attached to the outside of a window in urban apartments, allowing babies to get fresh air without the risk of falling. It was briefly popular but was eventually discontinued due to safety concerns.

Chapter 9: Inventions You Won't Believe Exist
Quirky Gadgets You Can Buy Today

- **The Ostrich Pillow**: This strange pillow allows you to take naps anywhere. Shaped like a large, cushioned helmet, it covers your head and hands, creating a cozy space for a quick nap on the go.
- **Smart Fork**: A gadget designed to help you eat slower, this fork vibrates when you're eating too fast. It tracks the speed of your bites and aims to promote healthier eating habits.
- **Pet Chatterbox**: This small device clips onto your pet's collar and plays pre-recorded messages in a "pet voice" as your dog or cat moves around. It's designed to entertain pet owners by imagining what their pets would say if they could talk.
- **Self-Stirring Mug**: Tired of stirring your coffee or tea? This mug has a built-in stirring mechanism at the bottom

that mixes your drink with the push of a button—perfect for the lazy coffee lover.
- **Roll-Up Keyboard**: Ideal for travelers or minimalists, this flexible keyboard can be rolled up and packed away. It connects to devices via Bluetooth and is surprisingly durable despite its soft, foldable design.

Famous Products with Unexpected Origins

- **Post-it Notes**: Post-it notes were invented by accident. **Spencer Silver**, a scientist at 3M, was trying to create a super-strong adhesive but ended up with one that was weak and reusable. Years later, it was used to create the sticky notes we know today.
- **Slinky**: The Slinky was invented by naval engineer **Richard James**, who was trying to develop springs for ship equipment. When one of the springs fell and "walked" across the floor, he realized its potential as a toy.
- **Coca-Cola**: Originally created as a medicinal tonic by pharmacist **John Stith Pemberton** in 1886, Coca-Cola was intended to treat ailments like headaches and fatigue. It wasn't until later that it became a popular soft drink.
- **Bubble Wrap**: Bubble wrap was originally designed as wallpaper! **Alfred Fielding** and **Marc Chavannes** were trying to create textured wallpaper but ended up with the plastic cushioning that's now used for packaging.
- **Corn Flakes**: Created by **John Harvey Kellogg**, corn flakes were originally intended as a health food to reduce people's sexual desire. The cereal became popular as a simple breakfast food, and its original purpose was forgotten.

Inventions That Flopped Spectacularly

- **The Segway**: Touted as a revolutionary mode of transportation, the Segway failed to take off as expected. Despite its innovative design, it was too expensive and impractical for everyday use, leading to disappointing sales.
- **New Coke (1985)**: Coca-Cola's attempt to reformulate its classic soda was met with public outrage. Consumers demanded the return of the original recipe, forcing the company to reintroduce it as "Coca-Cola Classic" within a few months.
- **Google Glass**: Google's attempt at wearable smart glasses generated hype but ultimately flopped due to concerns over privacy, high costs, and limited functionality. It failed to gain mainstream acceptance.
- **Colgate Frozen Dinners**: In the 1980s, toothpaste brand Colgate tried to expand into the frozen food market. Consumers were confused by the combination, associating the brand with minty toothpaste rather than meals.
- **The Apple Newton**: Released in the early 1990s, this personal digital assistant (PDA) was ahead of its time but struggled due to its unreliable handwriting recognition and high price. It was discontinued after a few years but paved the way for future innovations like the iPhone.

Innovative Ideas That Solved Odd Problems

- **The Pool Noodle**: This simple foam tube became an essential pool toy, but it wasn't invented as a toy at all. **Steve Hartman** originally designed it to help with insulation and construction, but its buoyancy made it perfect for floating.

- **LifeStraw**: This portable water filter allows people to drink directly from contaminated water sources. Originally created for use in emergencies and developing regions, it has become popular with hikers and travelers as well.
- **The Wacky Waving Inflatable Tube Man**: Invented by artist **Peter Minshall** for the 1996 Summer Olympics, this inflatable dancing figure was designed to entertain crowds. It later became an iconic advertising tool, grabbing attention outside car dealerships and stores.
- **The Clapper**: Designed as a way to turn lights on and off with a clap, the Clapper was a quirky invention that solved the problem of getting up to flip a switch. It became a popular novelty in the 1980s.
- **Velcro**: Inspired by the way burrs stick to clothing, Swiss engineer **George de Mestral** invented Velcro in 1941. The hook-and-loop fastener has since been used in everything from fashion to space travel.

Chapter 10: Language Wonders

Strange Idioms and Their Origins

- **"Break the ice"**: This idiom originated from the practice of breaking the ice in frozen waters to allow ships to pass. It now means to initiate a conversation or ease a tense situation.
- **"Bite the bullet"**: During early wars, soldiers would bite on bullets to endure the pain of surgery without anesthesia. Today, it means to face a difficult situation bravely.

- **"Cost an arm and a leg"**: This phrase comes from the 18th century when portrait artists charged more for paintings that included arms and legs. Today, it means something is very expensive.
- **"Raining cats and dogs"**: One theory is that this idiom comes from Norse mythology, where cats were associated with storms, and dogs were symbols of wind. It now describes heavy rain.
- **"Let the cat out of the bag"**: In medieval markets, unscrupulous traders would sell a pig in a sack, only to swap it with a less valuable cat. Today, it means to reveal a secret or let something slip.

Odd Languages and Writing Systems

- **Whistled Language (Silbo Gomero)**: On the Canary Island of La Gomera, an ancient whistled language is still in use. Silbo Gomero is used to communicate across the island's deep valleys, and its unique sounds allow complex messages to be conveyed.
- **Toki Pona**: Known as the world's smallest language, Toki Pona consists of only 120 words. It was created to simplify communication and encourage philosophical thinking, relying heavily on context.
- **Asemic Writing**: A form of writing with no specific meaning, asemic writing is purely abstract and artistic. It looks like text but cannot be read, blending visual art with the appearance of language.
- **Nüshu (China)**: Nüshu is a secret writing system created by women in China during the 19th century. It was used to communicate among women in a male-dominated society,

and its delicate, flowing script was passed down from generation to generation.
- **Pfeffel Code**: A unique writing system created by a Swiss-German artist in the early 20th century, the Pfeffel Code is based on colors rather than letters. Each letter of the alphabet is assigned a different color, creating colorful coded messages.

Words with No Translation

- **Torschlusspanik (German)**: Literally meaning "gate-closing panic," this word describes the fear of missing out on opportunities as time passes, especially as one ages.
- **Komorebi (Japanese)**: This beautiful word refers to the dappled sunlight that filters through the leaves of trees. It's a poetic way to describe the play of light and shadow in nature.
- **Gigil (Tagalog)**: Gigil refers to the irresistible urge to squeeze or pinch something unbearably cute. It's a feeling that often comes up when you see a baby or an adorable pet.
- **Saudade (Portuguese)**: Saudade is a deep emotional state of nostalgic longing for something or someone that is absent, often with the awareness that it may never return.
- **Tsundoku (Japanese)**: This word describes the act of acquiring books and letting them pile up without reading them. It reflects the love of books and the tendency to accumulate them faster than they can be read.

Unusual Facts About Language Creation

- **Esperanto**: Created by Polish-Jewish ophthalmologist **L. L. Zamenhof** in 1887, Esperanto was designed to be an easy-to-learn universal language, intended to promote peace and understanding between people from different nations. It's still spoken by around 2 million people today.
- **Dothraki (Game of Thrones)**: The fictional language of the Dothraki people was created by linguist **David J. Peterson** for the TV series *Game of Thrones*. It has over 3,000 words and is one of the most developed fictional languages in media.
- **Klingon (Star Trek)**: Developed by linguist **Marc Okrand** for the *Star Trek* universe, Klingon is a fully functional language with its own grammar and vocabulary. Dedicated fans have even translated works like *Hamlet* into Klingon.
- **Navajo Code Talkers**: During World War II, the U.S. military used the Navajo language as a code to communicate secret messages. The complex structure and limited speakers of the language made it nearly impossible for enemies to decipher.
- **Láadan (Feminist Science Fiction)**: Created by writer **Suzette Haden Elgin** in the 1980s for her science fiction novels, Láadan was a language designed to express the thoughts and feelings of women more clearly, emphasizing emotions and perceptions.

Surprising Word Origins

- **Quarantine**: This word comes from the Italian "quaranta giorni," meaning "forty days." Ships suspected of carrying the plague were isolated for 40 days before anyone could disembark, a practice that gave rise to the term.

- **Nightmare**: The word "mare" in Old English referred to an evil female spirit believed to suffocate sleepers. Combined with "night," it came to represent bad dreams caused by this supernatural being.
- **Salary**: The word "salary" comes from the Latin word "salarium," which was a payment made to Roman soldiers to buy salt, a valuable commodity at the time.
- **Alcohol**: Derived from the Arabic "al-kuḥl," which originally referred to a fine powder used for eyeliner (kohl). Over time, the meaning shifted to describe distilled substances, eventually coming to signify the drink we know today.
- **Sandwich**: The sandwich was named after **John Montagu**, the 4th Earl of Sandwich, who requested his meat be served between two slices of bread so he could continue gambling without needing utensils.

Chapter 11: Strange Superstitions

Common but Strange Superstitions

- **Breaking a Mirror Brings 7 Years of Bad Luck**: This superstition comes from ancient Rome, where people believed mirrors reflected not just one's appearance but also their soul. Damaging the mirror was thought to harm the soul and bring misfortune.
- **Knocking on Wood**: This practice originated in pagan times when people believed spirits lived in trees. By knocking on wood, they sought to invoke the protection of the spirits or prevent them from hearing a boast.
- **Friday the 13th**: Fear of this day likely stems from a combination of the number 13 being considered unlucky

and Friday's association with bad events, such as the crucifixion of Jesus. This superstition has led to widespread avoidance of the date.
- **Black Cats Crossing Your Path**: In medieval Europe, black cats were often associated with witches and evil omens. Seeing one cross your path was believed to bring bad luck, a belief that persists in many cultures today.
- **Opening an Umbrella Indoors**: This superstition dates back to Victorian England, where opening an umbrella inside was not only bad luck but also a physical hazard due to the spring-loaded mechanism of early umbrellas.

Weird Cultural Rituals for Good Luck

- **Throwing Plates on New Year's Eve (Denmark)**: In Denmark, it's tradition to throw plates at the doors of friends and family on New Year's Eve. The more broken plates you find on your doorstep, the more luck you'll have in the coming year.
- **Wearing Red Underwear (Italy)**: Italians believe that wearing red underwear on New Year's Eve brings good luck for the year ahead. Red is thought to symbolize fertility, prosperity, and passion.
- **Jumping Over Seven Waves (Brazil)**: On New Year's Eve, Brazilians head to the beach to jump over seven ocean waves. Each wave represents a wish, and this ritual is believed to bring good luck and protection for the upcoming year.
- **Money in Cake (Greece)**: Greeks celebrate the New Year by baking a cake called **Vasilopita**, which contains a hidden coin. Whoever finds the coin in their slice is said to have good fortune for the year.

- **Smashing a Pomegranate (Turkey)**: In Turkish culture, smashing a pomegranate on the ground at the entrance of your home is believed to bring prosperity and good luck for the new year. The more seeds that scatter, the luckier you'll be.

Historical Superstitions That Led to Bizarre Actions

- **Witch Hunts (16th-17th Century Europe and America)**: Fueled by superstition, the fear of witches led to the persecution and execution of thousands of people, mostly women, accused of witchcraft. The infamous **Salem witch trials** in 1692 saw 20 people executed and many more imprisoned.
- **Touching a King's Hand for Healing (Medieval Europe)**: In medieval Europe, it was believed that kings had the divine power to heal diseases such as scrofula (a form of tuberculosis) by touch. This belief, called the "Royal Touch," led to many seeking royal intervention for a cure.
- **Corpse Roads (Medieval Britain)**: In medieval Britain, superstitions around death were so strong that special "corpse roads" were created for transporting the dead to burial grounds. These roads avoided homes and settlements to prevent the spread of death's influence.
- **Placing Shoes in Walls (17th Century Europe)**: People in 17th-century Europe sometimes placed shoes inside the walls of houses during construction. This was believed to protect the home from evil spirits and bring good fortune to the inhabitants.
- **The Black Death and Flagellants (14th Century Europe)**: During the Black Death, religious groups called **flagellants** publicly whipped themselves as an act of

penance, believing that the plague was divine punishment. They thought self-inflicted suffering would spare them from the disease.

Famous Figures and Their Odd Superstitions

- **Napoleon Bonaparte**: The French emperor was famously afraid of black cats, believing them to be a bad omen. He avoided them at all costs, considering their presence a sign of impending misfortune.
- **Winston Churchill**: The British Prime Minister was highly superstitious about the number 13 and refused to sit in row 13 on airplanes. He also believed crossing one's legs while traveling brought bad luck.
- **Charles Dickens**: The famous author believed that sleeping with his head facing north helped his creativity and maintained his health. He was so particular about this that he would even rearrange his furniture in hotel rooms to ensure he was aligned with the north.
- **Franklin D. Roosevelt**: The U.S. President had a strong superstition about traveling on the 13th of any month and refused to sit with 13 people at a dinner table. He believed the number 13 was a bringer of bad luck.
- **Donald Trump**: The former U.S. president has a well-documented fear of germs, known as **mysophobia**. Trump avoids shaking hands whenever possible, believing it to be a source of disease transmission.

Unexplained Beliefs from Different Cultures

- **The Evil Eye (Mediterranean and Middle Eastern Cultures)**: The belief in the "evil eye" involves the idea that a person can cast a malevolent glare, causing harm or misfortune. People wear talismans, like the blue Nazar bead, to protect themselves from its effects.
- **The Wendigo (Indigenous North American Tribes)**: In certain Native American folklore, the Wendigo is a malevolent spirit associated with cold weather and famine. It was believed to possess people, turning them into cannibals driven by insatiable hunger.
- **Tabi-Tabi Po (Philippines)**: In Filipino culture, it's customary to say "tabi-tabi po" (meaning "excuse me") when passing through forests or grassy areas. This is believed to show respect to spirits, like elves or dwarves, that are thought to inhabit the land.
- **The Noppera-bō (Japan)**: This Japanese urban legend tells of a faceless ghost called the Noppera-bō, who appears as a normal person until its face suddenly disappears. The legend is tied to fears of deception and hidden dangers.
- **Throwing Salt Over Your Shoulder (Global)**: In many cultures, spilling salt is considered bad luck, dating back to ancient times when salt was a valuable commodity. To ward off bad luck, people throw a pinch of salt over their left shoulder to blind the devil who might be lurking behind them.

anings in Famous Paintings. Here's the next section:

Chapter 12: Eccentric Art and Literature
Hidden Meanings in Famous Paintings

- **The Last Supper (Leonardo da Vinci)**: Many believe that hidden messages are embedded in this iconic painting. Some theories suggest that the figure seated next to Jesus is not the Apostle John but Mary Magdalene, hinting at a deeper connection between her and Jesus.
- **The Arnolfini Portrait (Jan van Eyck)**: This painting is full of symbolic details. The small dog represents loyalty, while the single candle in the chandelier may symbolize the presence of God. The mirror in the background reflects additional figures, perhaps witnesses to the marriage.
- **The Creation of Adam (Michelangelo)**: Some scholars suggest that the shape surrounding God in Michelangelo's famous Sistine Chapel fresco resembles the human brain, implying that God's gift to Adam is not life, but intelligence and consciousness.
- **American Gothic (Grant Wood)**: Many interpret this painting as a satire of small-town American life, with its stiff, serious figures standing in front of a modest home. The pitchfork symbolizes labor and work ethic, while some see a hidden critique of Midwestern conservatism.
- **The Persistence of Memory (Salvador Dalí)**: Dalí's surrealist masterpiece, with its melting clocks, is often interpreted as a reflection on the fluidity of time and the fragility of memory. The limp, distorted objects challenge our usual perceptions of time's rigidity.

Strange Books and Their Backstories

- **The Voynich Manuscript**: This mysterious book, written in an unknown script and filled with strange, unidentifiable plants and astronomical symbols, has baffled scholars for

centuries. Despite extensive study, no one has been able to decode the manuscript's meaning.
- **Codex Seraphinianus**: Created by Italian artist **Luigi Serafini** in 1981, this book is written in a fictional language and features surreal, dreamlike illustrations. It's often considered one of the strangest art books ever made, with no clear narrative or explanation.
- **House of Leaves (Mark Z. Danielewski)**: This experimental horror novel tells the story of a family discovering that their house is bigger on the inside than on the outside. It's famous for its unconventional structure, with multiple narrators, footnotes, and sections printed upside down or in different fonts.
- **Finnegans Wake (James Joyce)**: One of the most challenging books in the English language, Joyce's novel is written in a stream-of-consciousness style, blending multiple languages, puns, and symbols. Its complex, dreamlike narrative has puzzled readers and scholars for decades.
- **The Book of Soyga**: Discovered in the 16th century by scholar **John Dee**, this book is filled with complex tables and encrypted text. Dee believed it contained powerful magical secrets, but it remained a mystery until its partial decoding in 2006.

Quirky Art Techniques and Styles

- **Pointillism**: Developed by **Georges Seurat** and **Paul Signac**, this technique involves creating images using tiny dots of pure color. From a distance, the dots blend together, but up close, they appear as separate, distinct points.

- **Drip Painting (Jackson Pollock)**: Pollock's "drip" or "action" painting style involves laying a canvas on the floor and pouring or splattering paint onto it. This spontaneous, chaotic method became a hallmark of Abstract Expressionism.
- **Surrealist Collage**: Artists like **Max Ernst** and **Hannah Höch** created surreal collages by cutting out images from magazines, books, and other sources, then rearranging them in bizarre and dreamlike ways. This technique challenged conventional representations of reality.
- **Anamorphosis**: A technique used to create distorted images that only appear normal when viewed from a specific angle or using a mirror. **Hans Holbein's** famous painting, *The Ambassadors*, includes a hidden skull that can only be seen from the side.
- **Hyperrealism**: Artists like **Ron Mueck** and **Chuck Close** take realism to an extreme, creating sculptures or paintings so detailed they look more real than reality itself. Mueck's oversized sculptures of human figures are particularly striking for their lifelike precision.

Famous Artists with Unusual Lives

- **Vincent van Gogh**: Known for his emotional paintings and use of vibrant color, Van Gogh struggled with mental illness throughout his life. He famously cut off part of his own ear and spent time in a psychiatric hospital, where he painted some of his most famous works, including *Starry Night*.
- **Salvador Dalí**: The eccentric surrealist painter was known for his flamboyant personality and outlandish behavior. He once showed up to a lecture in a diving suit, claiming he

was "diving into the depths of the human mind." Dalí's bizarre public appearances were as famous as his dreamlike art.
- **Frida Kahlo**: Kahlo's life was marked by physical pain and personal hardship. After a bus accident left her with lifelong injuries, she turned to painting to express her emotions. Her surreal, often autobiographical work reflects her struggles with identity, love, and suffering.
- **Leonardo da Vinci**: A true Renaissance man, Leonardo's interests spanned art, science, anatomy, and engineering. He was left-handed, wrote in mirror script, and often filled his notebooks with inventions and anatomical sketches that were centuries ahead of their time.
- **Georgia O'Keeffe**: Best known for her large-scale paintings of flowers and Southwestern landscapes, O'Keeffe led a reclusive life in the deserts of New Mexico. She was deeply connected to the landscape, and her solitary lifestyle influenced her unique artistic vision.

Odd and Controversial Literary Works

- **Lolita (Vladimir Nabokov)**: This 1955 novel, about an older man's obsession with a 12-year-old girl, has been both lauded for its literary merit and criticized for its disturbing subject matter. Despite the controversy, *Lolita* is considered a classic of modern literature.
- **Naked Lunch (William S. Burroughs)**: Burroughs' 1959 novel is an experimental, non-linear narrative that explores drug addiction, control, and the human psyche. Its explicit content led to several obscenity trials, but it has since been recognized as a groundbreaking work of the Beat Generation.

- **Ulysses (James Joyce)**: When it was first published in 1922, *Ulysses* was banned in several countries for its explicit content and stream-of-consciousness style. Today, it's celebrated as one of the most important modernist novels ever written.
- **The Satanic Verses (Salman Rushdie)**: Rushdie's 1988 novel caused widespread protests in the Islamic world for its perceived blasphemy against Islam. The controversy escalated to the point where Iran's Supreme Leader issued a fatwa calling for Rushdie's assassination.
- **The Story of the Eye (Georges Bataille)**: Written in 1928, this surreal and erotic novel shocked readers with its graphic content. It remains controversial for its depictions of taboo subjects, blending eroticism with themes of death and violence.

Chapter 13: Space Mysteries and Oddities

Unusual Planets and Moons in the Solar System

- **Venus**: Despite being Earth's "twin" in size, Venus is a hellish world with surface temperatures hot enough to melt lead. Its thick atmosphere, composed mainly of carbon dioxide, creates a runaway greenhouse effect that traps heat and makes it the hottest planet in the solar system.
- **Io (Moon of Jupiter)**: Io is the most volcanically active body in the solar system. Its surface is covered in lava lakes and geysers of sulfur, giving it an otherworldly, colorful appearance of reds, yellows, and whites.

- **Titan (Moon of Saturn)**: Titan has lakes and rivers, but they're not made of water—they're filled with liquid methane and ethane. This moon is the only place in the solar system, aside from Earth, with stable bodies of liquid on its surface.
- **Neptune**: Neptune's atmosphere features some of the fastest winds in the solar system, with speeds reaching up to 1,200 miles per hour (2,000 kilometers per hour). These winds whip around dark storm systems, similar to Jupiter's Great Red Spot.
- **Haumea**: This dwarf planet, located beyond Neptune, has an elongated, egg-like shape due to its rapid rotation. It completes one full spin in just four hours, causing it to be stretched out, unlike the more spherical planets.

Bizarre Space Phenomena

- **Black Holes**: These mysterious objects have such immense gravitational pull that nothing, not even light, can escape. Black holes warp spacetime, and their event horizons mark the boundary beyond which nothing can return. Some theories suggest black holes could be gateways to other dimensions.
- **Dark Matter**: Although it makes up about 85% of the universe's mass, dark matter is invisible and undetectable by current technology. It doesn't emit or absorb light, but its existence is inferred through its gravitational effects on galaxies and other cosmic structures.
- **Neutron Stars**: After a massive star collapses, it may form a neutron star, an incredibly dense object made mostly of neutrons. A teaspoon of neutron star material would weigh

billions of tons. Some neutron stars emit beams of radiation as they spin, creating the "lighthouse" effect of pulsars.
- **The Great Attractor**: This gravitational anomaly is pulling galaxies, including our Milky Way, toward it at millions of miles per hour. However, its exact nature is unknown because it lies in a region of space obscured by the Milky Way's dust and gas.
- **The Cosmic Microwave Background**: This faint glow of radiation is the afterglow of the Big Bang, providing a snapshot of the early universe. The CMB is one of the strongest pieces of evidence supporting the Big Bang theory, but it also raises questions about the uniformity of the universe.

Quirky Astronaut Facts

- **Buzz Aldrin's Communion on the Moon**: Before stepping onto the lunar surface, astronaut Buzz Aldrin quietly took communion. He brought a small communion kit with him and held a private ceremony to give thanks in his own way before the historic moonwalk.
- **Charlie Duke's Family Photo on the Moon**: Apollo 16 astronaut Charlie Duke left a small photograph of his family on the moon. The photo, encased in plastic, is still there, likely faded or degraded by the harsh lunar environment.
- **Space Smells Like Burnt Steak**: Many astronauts describe the smell of space as being similar to burnt metal or steak. This odor clings to their suits after spacewalks and has been noted by astronauts aboard the International Space Station.
- **A Tardigrade's Space Adventure**: In 2007, scientists sent **tardigrades**, microscopic creatures known for their

extreme survival abilities, into space. The tardigrades survived the vacuum of space and the intense solar radiation, proving their toughness even in extraterrestrial environments.
- **Astronauts Grow Taller in Space**: In microgravity, astronauts' spines expand, making them grow up to 2 inches taller while in space. Unfortunately, they shrink back to their normal height once they return to Earth's gravity.

Strange Historical Beliefs About Space

- **The Celestial Spheres (Ancient Greece)**: Ancient Greek astronomers believed that the planets and stars were fixed in crystal spheres that revolved around the Earth. This geocentric model dominated Western thought for centuries, with each sphere representing a different heavenly body.
- **The Hollow Moon Theory**: In the 1970s, some conspiracy theorists proposed that the Moon was hollow and possibly an alien spacecraft. This theory arose after Apollo mission data suggested the Moon "rang like a bell" during seismic activity, which they misinterpreted as evidence of hollowness.
- **Lunar Lunacy (Medieval Europe)**: People once believed that the phases of the Moon could influence human behavior, particularly causing madness. The term "lunatic" comes from the Latin word for "moon" (luna), reflecting the belief that the Moon could drive people insane.
- **Martian Canals**: In the late 19th century, astronomer **Percival Lowell** famously observed what he believed were canals on Mars, built by intelligent beings. While these turned out to be optical illusions, his work sparked public fascination with the possibility of life on Mars.

- **The Sun as a Chariot (Ancient Egypt and Greece)**: Ancient civilizations believed the Sun was a god traveling across the sky in a chariot. In Egypt, the Sun god **Ra** was thought to sail through the sky in a boat, while in Greece, the Sun was personified as **Helios**, riding a fiery chariot.

Space Exploration Oddities

- **Apollo 12's Lightning Strike**: Just 36 seconds after launch, the Apollo 12 spacecraft was struck by lightning—twice. Despite the electrical failure, quick thinking by the mission team saved the mission, and the astronauts continued on to the Moon.
- **The "Lost" Cosmonauts**: Some conspiracy theories suggest that the Soviet Union launched cosmonauts into space before Yuri Gagarin, but that these missions ended in failure and were covered up. There is no confirmed evidence of these so-called "lost cosmonauts."
- **The Space Pen Controversy**: NASA famously used the "space pen," which could write in zero gravity, underwater, and at extreme temperatures. Contrary to popular myth, NASA did not waste millions developing the pen—**Paul C. Fisher** invented it independently and sold it to NASA for just a few dollars.
- **Laika's Hidden Story**: Laika, the first dog to orbit Earth aboard Sputnik 2, was long believed to have survived several days in space. However, it was later revealed that she died just hours after launch due to overheating, making her story a tragic milestone in space exploration.
- **Astronauts on the Moon Heard Music**: During the Apollo 10 mission, astronauts orbiting the Moon reported hearing strange "whistling" sounds coming through their radios.

NASA later explained that this was likely radio interference, but the eerie "space music" remains one of the more curious moments in space exploration history.

Chapter 14: Unexplained Phenomena

Famous Unsolved Mysteries

- **The Bermuda Triangle**: This area of the Atlantic Ocean, bounded by Miami, Bermuda, and Puerto Rico, is infamous for the mysterious disappearance of ships and airplanes. While some attribute these incidents to unusual weather patterns or magnetic anomalies, no definitive explanation has been proven.
- **The Dyatlov Pass Incident**: In 1959, nine Russian hikers died under strange circumstances in the Ural Mountains. Their tent was found slashed open from the inside, and some of the bodies showed signs of trauma, including severe internal injuries, but with no external wounds. Theories range from an avalanche to military testing, yet the true cause remains unknown.
- **The Wow! Signal**: In 1977, astronomer **Jerry Ehman** detected a strong radio signal from space while working at Ohio State University's Big Ear radio telescope. The signal, known as the "Wow! Signal," lasted 72 seconds and has never been explained, leading to speculation about its extraterrestrial origin.
- **The Mary Celeste**: In 1872, the Mary Celeste, a merchant ship, was found adrift in the Atlantic Ocean with no crew aboard. The ship was intact, and all the crew's belongings

were left behind, but the crew members were never found, and their fate remains a mystery.
- **The Taos Hum**: In the small town of Taos, New Mexico, residents have reported hearing a persistent low-frequency hum that no one has been able to explain. Despite investigations, the source of the sound remains unidentified, leaving scientists and locals baffled.

Strange Natural Phenomena

- **Ball Lightning**: A rare phenomenon, ball lightning appears as glowing, floating orbs of light during thunderstorms. These orbs can vary in size and color, and while there are numerous eyewitness reports, the exact cause of ball lightning remains a mystery to scientists.
- **Aurora Borealis (Northern Lights)**: While we know the northern lights are caused by charged particles from the sun interacting with Earth's magnetic field, the dazzling light displays still seem otherworldly. Ancient cultures believed they were messages from the gods or spirits.
- **Red Rain (Kerala, India, 2001)**: In 2001, red-colored rain fell over the Indian state of Kerala. Initially thought to be the result of dust or algae, further analysis suggested the presence of unusual biological cells, sparking theories about extraterrestrial origins. However, the exact cause remains unclear.
- **The Hessdalen Lights (Norway)**: In the Hessdalen Valley, mysterious floating lights have appeared regularly since the 1930s. These glowing orbs of light move erratically across the sky, and despite extensive scientific research, no one has been able to explain their origin.

- **The Sailing Stones (Death Valley, USA)**: In Death Valley's Racetrack Playa, large rocks appear to move across the desert floor, leaving trails behind them. These "sailing stones" have baffled scientists for decades. Recent research suggests that thin sheets of ice push the stones, but the phenomenon is still not fully understood.

Mysterious Ancient Artifacts

- **The Antikythera Mechanism**: Discovered in a shipwreck off the coast of Greece in 1901, this ancient device, dating back to around 100 BCE, is believed to be an early analog computer. Its complexity, used to predict astronomical positions, baffles historians, as no similar technology was known to exist for another thousand years.
- **The Baghdad Battery**: Found near Baghdad, this artifact dates back to around 250 BCE. Consisting of a clay jar, copper tube, and iron rod, it's believed to have been capable of producing electricity. Its purpose, however, remains a mystery—some speculate it was used for electroplating or religious rituals.
- **The Piri Reis Map**: Created in 1513 by the Ottoman admiral **Piri Reis**, this map shows the coastlines of South America, Africa, and even Antarctica (which wasn't officially discovered until centuries later). How Piri Reis had access to such detailed geographical knowledge remains a mystery.
- **The Shroud of Turin**: This linen cloth bears the faint image of a man's face and body and is believed by some to be the burial shroud of Jesus Christ. While radiocarbon dating suggests it's a medieval forgery, the mystery of how the image was created still puzzles scientists.

- **The Voynich Manuscript**: Written in an unknown language or code and filled with strange, unidentifiable plants and astronomical drawings, this 15th-century book has baffled scholars for centuries. Despite extensive research, no one has successfully deciphered its meaning.

Unexplained Disappearances

- **The Disappearance of Amelia Earhart**: In 1937, famed aviator **Amelia Earhart** vanished while attempting to fly around the world. Despite extensive search efforts, no trace of her or her plane was ever found, leading to numerous theories ranging from a crash at sea to capture by enemy forces.
- **The Lost Colony of Roanoke**: In 1587, English settlers established a colony on Roanoke Island in what is now North Carolina. When supply ships returned three years later, the colony was deserted, with the only clue being the word "CROATOAN" carved into a tree. The fate of the settlers remains a mystery.
- **The Flannan Isles Lighthouse Keepers**: In 1900, three lighthouse keepers on the remote Flannan Isles off the coast of Scotland vanished without a trace. Their disappearance remains unsolved, with theories ranging from a rogue wave to supernatural causes.
- **The MV Joyita**: In 1955, the MV Joyita, a merchant vessel, was found drifting in the South Pacific with no crew aboard. The ship was in disrepair, and all lifeboats were missing, but no signs of struggle or distress were found. The fate of the crew remains unknown.
- **The Bennington Triangle**: This area in Vermont became infamous between 1945 and 1950 when five people

mysteriously disappeared. Despite extensive searches, no trace of the missing individuals was ever found, and the disappearances remain unexplained.

Paranormal Events That Defy Explanation

- **The Enfield Poltergeist (1977)**: In a small London suburb, the Hodgson family reported terrifying paranormal activity in their home, including furniture moving on its own, strange voices, and levitating children. While some believe it was a hoax, witnesses, including police officers, claimed to have seen unexplainable events.
- **The Bell Witch (1817-1821)**: The Bell family in Tennessee was reportedly haunted by a malevolent spirit that tormented them for years. The "Bell Witch" allegedly spoke to family members, predicted future events, and even caused the death of **John Bell**, the head of the household.
- **The Phoenix Lights (1997)**: Thousands of people in Arizona reported seeing strange lights in a V-shaped formation moving silently across the night sky. The event remains one of the most well-documented UFO sightings, though no official explanation has been provided.
- **The Amityville Horror (1974)**: After the brutal murder of the DeFeo family, the house in Amityville, New York, gained notoriety when the Lutz family claimed to experience intense paranormal activity. Their accounts included strange noises, foul smells, and ghostly apparitions, though skeptics question the validity of the claims.
- **The Mothman (1966-1967)**: In Point Pleasant, West Virginia, numerous sightings of a mysterious winged creature known as the "Mothman" were reported. The

sightings culminated in the collapse of the Silver Bridge, which some believe was connected to the creature's appearance. The Mothman legend continues to captivate paranormal enthusiasts.

Chapter 15: Bizarre Sports and Games
Unusual Sporting Events and Traditions

- **Cheese Rolling (England)**: Every year, people gather in Gloucester, England, to participate in the **Cooper's Hill Cheese-Rolling and Wake**, where competitors chase a large round of cheese down a steep hill. The first person to reach the bottom wins the cheese, but injuries are common due to the rough terrain.
- **Wife Carrying (Finland)**: Originating in Finland, the **Wife Carrying World Championship** involves male competitors racing through an obstacle course while carrying their wives on their backs. The winner receives the wife's weight in beer as a prize.
- **Underwater Hockey (Global)**: Also known as **Octopush**, this sport is played on the bottom of a swimming pool with players using small sticks to push a puck toward the opposing team's goal. It combines the strategy of hockey with the challenge of breath control.
- **Toe Wrestling (England)**: In Derbyshire, England, toe wrestling is a popular sport where competitors lock toes and attempt to pin their opponent's foot down. It's similar to arm wrestling but much quirkier.

- **Extreme Ironing (Global)**: Combining the thrill of extreme sports with the mundane task of ironing, competitors take their ironing boards to unusual locations—such as mountain tops, underwater, or while skydiving—and iron clothing in extreme conditions.

Obscure Sports That Are Surprisingly Popular

- **Kabaddi (South Asia)**: This team sport is especially popular in India, Bangladesh, and Iran. Players take turns trying to tag opponents while holding their breath and chanting "kabaddi" repeatedly, all while avoiding being tackled by the opposing team.
- **Bossaball (Global)**: A mix of volleyball, soccer, gymnastics, and capoeira, Bossaball is played on an inflatable court with a trampoline in the middle. Players use any part of their body to hit the ball over the net, and acrobatic flips are encouraged.
- **Sepak Takraw (Southeast Asia)**: This fast-paced sport is similar to volleyball, but players use their feet, knees, and head to kick a rattan ball over the net. It requires incredible agility and is highly popular in countries like Thailand and Malaysia.
- **Chess Boxing (Global)**: In this unusual hybrid sport, competitors alternate between rounds of chess and boxing. Victory can be achieved either by checkmate or knockout, blending mental and physical prowess.
- **Cycle Ball (Europe)**: Also known as "radball," this sport involves two players on bicycles attempting to hit a ball into the opponent's goal using only the wheels of their bikes. It's a combination of soccer and cycling and is especially popular in Austria and Germany.

Weird World Records in Sports

- **Longest Tennis Match**: In 2010, **John Isner** and **Nicolas Mahut** played the longest tennis match in history at Wimbledon, lasting 11 hours and 5 minutes over the course of three days. Isner eventually won with a score of 70-68 in the fifth set.
- **Most Marathon Finishes in a Year**: **Ricardo Abad**, a Spanish ultramarathoner, set a world record by running 607 marathons in 607 consecutive days from 2010 to 2012. His incredible endurance earned him worldwide recognition.
- **Fastest 100m Sprint on Stilts**: In 2010, **Saimir Strati** set the world record for the fastest 100-meter sprint on stilts, completing the run in just 14.1 seconds. The record combines athleticism and balance on an unusual platform.
- **Most Skipping Rope Jumps on One Leg**: Japanese athlete **Ayumi Niekawa** set a world record in 2017 by performing 11,017 skipping rope jumps on one leg in a single hour, showcasing incredible stamina and focus.
- **Heaviest Weight Lifted with an Eyelid**: In 2009, **Zhou Chengli** from China lifted a 16.5-pound (7.5 kg) weight using only his eyelid. This unusual record combines strength with an extraordinary tolerance for pain.

The Most Unusual Games Played Around the World

- **Conkers (UK)**: Played with horse chestnuts (called conkers), this traditional British game involves two players taking turns striking each other's conker with a string. The goal is to break your opponent's conker while keeping yours intact.

- **Buzkashi (Central Asia)**: Known as one of the world's most intense sports, Buzkashi involves players on horseback attempting to drag a headless goat carcass into a goal. It's the national sport of Afghanistan and requires exceptional riding skills.
- **Eukonkanto (Wife Carrying, Finland)**: In this game, men race through obstacle courses while carrying their wives in various positions, such as "Estonian style," where the wife hangs upside-down on the husband's back. The winner receives the wife's weight in beer.
- **Pato (Argentina)**: Argentina's national sport, Pato, is a combination of basketball and polo. Played on horseback, the game involves players throwing a ball with handles into a hoop while riding at high speeds.
- **Kubb (Sweden)**: Sometimes called "Viking Chess," Kubb is an outdoor lawn game where players attempt to knock over wooden blocks (kubbs) by throwing wooden batons. The game is won by toppling the king block in the center of the field.

Quirky Competitions and Their Origins

- **The World Beard and Moustache Championships**: This competition, which takes place in different locations around the world, celebrates elaborate facial hair. Categories include full beards, styled mustaches, and freestyle designs. The competition began in Germany and has since gained global popularity.
- **Air Guitar World Championships**: Held annually in Finland, this quirky competition invites participants to perform exaggerated air guitar solos in front of a live

audience. The idea is to promote world peace through "airness" and rock 'n' roll spirit.
- **Bog Snorkeling (Wales)**: Competitors swim through muddy, water-filled trenches in a peat bog while wearing snorkels and flippers. Originating in Llanwrtyd Wells, Wales, the event attracts adventurous athletes and is part of the town's annual sports festival.
- **The Stone Skimming Championship (Scotland)**: Held on the island of Easdale, Scotland, this competition challenges participants to skim stones across a quarry filled with water. The goal is to see how many times the stone can skip across the surface.
- **Mobile Phone Throwing (Finland)**: Started in Finland in 2000, this competition allows participants to throw old mobile phones as far as they can. It's both a quirky sport and a form of recycling, combining humor with a practical environmental message.

Chapter 16: Human Curiosities
Unusual Body Modifications

- **Stretched Earlobes**: Practiced by various cultures worldwide, the process of stretching earlobes involves gradually enlarging the ear piercing over time. In some cultures, such as the Maasai in Kenya, this symbolizes beauty and social status.
- **Corset Piercing**: This extreme body modification involves a series of piercings along the back or sides, often laced with ribbons to resemble a corset. While mostly temporary, some enthusiasts keep the piercings long-term for aesthetic purposes.

- **Neck Elongation (Kayan Tribe, Myanmar)**: Women of the Kayan tribe traditionally wear brass rings around their necks, starting in childhood. Over time, the rings push down the collarbone and compress the ribcage, giving the appearance of a longer neck, which is considered a mark of beauty.
- **Scarification**: In this modification, the skin is intentionally scarred using tools like knives or branding irons to create raised patterns. Scarification is practiced in various African and indigenous cultures as a rite of passage or as a mark of identity.
- **Tongue Splitting**: Popular in the body modification community, tongue splitting involves cutting the tongue down the middle to create a forked appearance, similar to a snake's tongue. The procedure is often done for aesthetic or personal expression reasons.

Strange Medical Anomalies

- **Hypertrichosis (Werewolf Syndrome)**: This rare condition causes excessive hair growth all over the body, including the face. It can be congenital or acquired, and individuals with hypertrichosis have been part of circus sideshows in the past due to their unusual appearance.
- **Polydactyly**: People with polydactyly are born with extra fingers or toes. While these extra digits are usually functional, they are often surgically removed in childhood for cosmetic reasons.
- **Stone Man Syndrome (Fibrodysplasia Ossificans Progressiva)**: A rare genetic disorder where soft tissues like muscles, tendons, and ligaments gradually turn into bone.

Over time, this "second skeleton" severely limits movement and can make daily activities nearly impossible.
- **Alien Hand Syndrome**: This neurological condition causes one hand to move involuntarily, often performing actions without the person's control. It can be caused by brain injuries, strokes, or surgeries, and those affected sometimes describe their hand as having a "mind of its own."
- **The Elephant Man (Joseph Merrick)**: Joseph Merrick, known as the "Elephant Man," suffered from severe physical deformities caused by a combination of conditions, including Proteus syndrome. His disfigurement made him famous, but his case also highlighted the mistreatment of people with physical anomalies in the 19th century.

Amazing Human Feats of Endurance

- **Wim Hof (The Iceman)**: Known for his ability to withstand extreme cold, **Wim Hof** has set numerous world records, including climbing Mount Kilimanjaro in shorts and running a half-marathon above the Arctic Circle barefoot. He credits his endurance to breathing techniques and cold exposure training.
- **Dean Karnazes (Ultramarathon Runner)**: Karnazes is famous for running 50 marathons in 50 U.S. states in 50 consecutive days. He has also run non-stop for over 350 miles without sleep, demonstrating superhuman levels of stamina and endurance.
- **David Blaine (Endurance Artist)**: The illusionist and endurance artist has performed several high-profile endurance stunts, including being buried alive for seven days and surviving 44 days suspended in a transparent box

without food. His feats often blur the line between magic and extreme physical endurance.
- **Göran Kropp**: This Swedish adventurer cycled from Sweden to the base of Mount Everest and then climbed the mountain without supplemental oxygen or Sherpa support. His journey was one of the most remarkable displays of both physical and mental endurance.
- **Mauro Prosperi**: During the Marathon des Sables, a grueling six-day ultramarathon across the Sahara Desert, Prosperi became lost in a sandstorm and survived nine days in the desert by drinking his own urine and eating bats. His survival story is a testament to human resilience.

Unusual Human Talents

- **Stephen Wiltshire (Photographic Memory)**: Stephen Wiltshire is an artist known for his extraordinary ability to draw detailed cityscapes entirely from memory. After a brief helicopter ride, he can recreate vast cities like Tokyo or New York with astonishing accuracy, down to the number of windows on buildings.
- **Isao Machii (Superhuman Reflexes)**: This Japanese sword master holds multiple world records for his incredible reflexes, including slicing a pellet in mid-air fired at over 200 mph. His samurai-like skills are so precise that scientists have studied his brain to understand his lightning-fast reaction time.
- **Ben Underwood (Human Echolocation)**: Blind since childhood, Ben Underwood taught himself echolocation, using clicks of his tongue to navigate and "see" his surroundings. His remarkable ability to detect objects

through sound allowed him to ride a bike and play basketball without assistance.
- **Daniel Tammet (Mathematical Savant)**: Tammet has an exceptional ability to memorize and perform complex mathematical calculations. He once recited the number pi to 22,514 decimal places, a feat that took him over five hours. He also speaks 11 languages and can learn new languages in a matter of days.
- **Kim Peek (The Real Rain Man)**: The inspiration for the film *Rain Man*, Kim Peek had an extraordinary ability to memorize vast amounts of information. He could recall the contents of 12,000 books, reading each page in just a few seconds, and could process different pages with each eye simultaneously.

Bizarre Human Behaviors

- **Pica**: People with pica have an intense craving to eat non-food substances like dirt, chalk, or hair. This condition, often associated with nutritional deficiencies or psychological disorders, can lead to serious health issues depending on what's ingested.
- **Trichotillomania**: This disorder causes people to compulsively pull out their own hair, often from their scalp, eyelashes, or eyebrows. It's considered a body-focused repetitive behavior and can lead to noticeable hair loss.
- **Latah (Southeast Asia)**: Latah is a condition found primarily in Southeast Asia where individuals exhibit exaggerated responses to startling stimuli, such as mimicking others or following commands automatically. The behavior can seem involuntary and has deep cultural associations.

- **Paris Syndrome (Tourists in Paris)**: A bizarre psychological phenomenon, Paris Syndrome affects some tourists, particularly from Japan, who experience severe disappointment and shock upon realizing that Paris doesn't match their idealized expectations. Symptoms include anxiety, dizziness, and hallucinations.
- **Jerusalem Syndrome**: A psychological condition in which visitors to Jerusalem become overwhelmed by religious experiences and start believing they are biblical figures or have a divine mission. The condition can lead to strange behavior, such as preaching in public or attempting to enact religious prophecies.

Conclusion: The Endless Curiosity of the World

As we reach the end of **"The Book of Unusual Knowledge,"** it becomes clear that our world—and the universe beyond—is filled with countless wonders, mysteries, and curiosities. From the strange and fascinating history of human inventions to the awe-inspiring phenomena of outer space, the richness of the unknown fuels our imagination and our quest for learning.

The trivia and facts we've uncovered serve as a reminder that there is always something new to discover, even in the most unexpected places. Whether it's an unusual sport, an unsolved mystery, or an extraordinary human talent, these oddities ignite our curiosity and encourage us to look deeper.

But what truly connects all of these facts is the innate human desire to understand the world around us. It's a desire that spans centuries and cultures—manifesting in art, science, superstition, and even the strange quirks of daily life. Our quest for knowledge is never-ending, and with each new discovery, we find more questions to ask and more mysteries to solve.

In a world where the extraordinary is often hidden in plain sight, it's important to stay curious, to keep asking questions, and to embrace the oddities that make life so wonderfully unpredictable. Whether you're chasing cheese down a hill, marveling at the stars, or wondering about ancient artifacts, let your curiosity guide you.

And as you close this book, remember: the pursuit of unusual knowledge is never truly finished. There is always more to explore, more to learn, and more to be fascinated by. The world's mysteries are endless, and that's what makes the journey of discovery so rewarding.

Printed in Great Britain
by Amazon